SEA OTTERS

A SURVIVAL STORY

Foreword by **Dame Judi Dench** and **David F. Mills**

Text and photographs by

ISABELLE GROC

ORCA BOOK PUBLISHERS

Library and Archives Canada Cataloguing in Publication
Title: Sea otters: a survival story / text and photographs by Isabelle Groc.
Names: Groc, Isabelle, author, photographer.
Description: Series statement: Orca wild | Includes bibliographical references and index.
Identifiers: Canadiana (print) 20190173319 | Canadiana (ebook) 20190173327 |
ISBN 9781459817371 (hardcover) | ISBN 9781459817388 (PDF) | ISBN 9781459817395 (EPUB)
Subjects: LCSH: Sea otter—Juvenile literature. | LCSH: Sea otter—Conservation—Juvenile literature.
Classification: LCC QL737.C25 G76 2020 | DDC j599.769/5—dc23

Library of Congress Control Number: 2019947362
Simultaneously published in Canada and the United States in 2020

Summary: Part of the nonfiction Orca Wild series for middle readers, this book looks at the important role
sea otters play in ecosystems. Readers will learn about the history of sea otters, their recovery from near extinction
and how to conserve the species for the future. Illustrated with photos by the photojournalist author.

*Orca Book Publishers is committed to reducing the consumption of nonrenewable resources in the making
of our books. We make every effort to use materials that support a sustainable future.*

Orca Book Publishers gratefully acknowledges the support for its publishing programs provided by
the following agencies: the Government of Canada, the Canada Council for the Arts and the Province
of British Columbia through the BC Arts Council and the Book Publishing Tax Credit.

Front cover photos: Isabelle Groc

Edited by Sarah N. Harvey
Design by Dahlia Yuen

ORCA BOOK PUBLISHERS
orcabook.com

Printed and bound in South Korea.

23 22 21 20 • 4 3 2 1

Sea otters have the densest fur of any
mammal. Unlike other marine mammals
they do not have any blubber, so they
depend on their thick, water-resistant
fur to stay warm in the cold water.

To my parents, who introduced me to the wonders of the sea.

Contents

LIVING WITH SEA OTTERS 79

Foreword

MY LOVE AFFAIR WITH OTTERS began in the very early seventies when my husband, Michael Williams, and I were touring Australia with the Royal Shakespeare Company. There we were bewitched by the Asian small-clawed otter, and subsequently, on our return home we adopted two at the Cotswold Wildlife Park. Much later, in 2004, I was filming in Vancouver, and on one memorable day I was taken to see the sea otters, who are considerably larger than their Asian cousins. For hours, it seemed, I watched enthralled as two of them floated on their backs, arms linked, while one slept and the other steered and kept watch—an unforgettable experience!

Many years later, every time I drove past the British Wildlife Centre, which is only five miles away from me, I would say, "That man in there's got otters!" Eventually I visited the centre and discovered to my delight that "that man in there" did indeed have otters!

When I read Isabelle's book, I discovered that the fur trade of the 18th and 19th centuries brought sea otters to near extinction. Today they are coming back, thanks to the protections that have been put in place. Scientists have learned that when sea otters return, they have a tremendous impact on the ecosystem, as a keystone species.

In this beautiful book, Isabelle tells us an important story, one that gives us hope. The story of the sea otter demonstrates that conservation efforts can make a difference and bring a species back from the brink. Young people will be encouraged to see that positive changes can happen and that we can all do something to help preserve our planet. Hope is much needed today!

—Dame Judi Dench

I CERTAINLY DO HAVE OTTERS at the British Wildlife Centre. Ours, of course, are our own native European otter (*Lutra lutra*), which was on the brink of extinction in Britain in the mid-sixties. Through a huge national program of cleaning up our polluted waterways, restoring habitat and banning hunting, coupled with a captive breeding and release program, we can now safely say that there are otters once again in every county in Britain—a truly remarkable success story!

Although European river otters and sea otters are quite different, they share a similar story: with hope, care and the persistence of people who have not given up in different parts of the world, these two species have been saved from extinction.

In Isabelle's book you will find everything you need to know about the sea otter, beautifully illustrated by her amazing photographs. We can't recommend it highly enough!

—David F. Mills,
MBE, founder and owner
of the British Wildlife Centre

A northern sea otter in Alaska keeps its paws out of the cold water to conserve heat.

Introduction

When I first saw shiny dark heads moving on the surface of the water while I was walking a shoreline on Vancouver Island in British Columbia, I was not sure what I was seeing. I thought they were pieces of floating *kelp*, the large brown seaweed often seen on the west coast of North America. I reached for my binoculars. What I saw was unexpected and magical—about 120 sea otters holding on to each other, floating gently on the water and resting.

Today, people can enjoy watching sea otters on the Pacific coast. This was not always the case, and every time I spot a sea otter, I am reminded that these animals are incredible survivors.

The sea otter symbolizes the large impacts—both positive and negative—that humans can have on wildlife and *ecosystems*. Sea otters are the smallest marine mammals in North America. Because they have no fat to keep them warm in the cold waters of the North Pacific,

A raft of male sea otters in British Columbia. Females and their pups form separate rafts from males, and the rafts vary in size.

they rely on their luxuriant fur coats to survive. But their fur has also been a death sentence. Sea otters were hunted for their valuable pelts to the point of near *extinction* in the maritime fur trade in the 18th and 19th centuries. Fewer than 2,000 sea otters were left at the end of the fur trade. Luckily, a few small *remnant populations* managed to survive in remote places, and in the early 20th century laws were passed to protect the animals from being killed or harmed. Following active conservation efforts, sea-otter populations have started to recover.

Today sea otters are one of the most widely studied animals in the world. They have shown us that they are able to survive and thrive. They also intrigue us in many ways. After all, they are one of the few non-primate *species* known to use tools. Their feeding behavior also has broader implications, affecting the entire ecosystem.

Sea otters make a big difference in the world, and the scientists who study them are constantly surprised by what these extraordinary creatures can do. They are truly nature's ecosystem engineers. Sea otters have demonstrated not only their amazing ability to survive in the face of near extermination by humans, but also their true powers. Their remarkable skills as a *predator* and huge appetites give them the capacity to profoundly transform the environment everywhere they swim, leading to the rebirth of kelp forests and other *habitats* in North America. They show us—the humans who came close to destroying them—how important it is to deal with some of the major environmental challenges we face today, including *climate change*, habitat destruction and *pollution*.

In this book you will learn about the sea otters' unique existence and how they leave their mark (or paw print) on the environment in both obvious and subtle ways. Sea otters teach us that everything in the ecosystem is connected, from kelp to *seagrass*, crabs to bald eagles, wolves to humans. And they show us how complex the return of a top predator can be.

You will meet the scientists studying sea otters, and you will find out about some of the methods they use to learn about these animals. As resilient as they are, sea otters are also seriously threatened in today's world. The International Union for Conservation of Nature Red List of Threatened Species has classified them as "endangered." Learning how to live with sea otters and ensure their long-term survival is one of the keys to maintaining a rich, complex ecosystem.

A northern sea-otter mother carries her pup on her chest in Alaska for the first two months of its life. She will constantly groom the pup and protect it from the cold water.

A northern sea otter is resting in kelp in Checleset Bay, BC, where sea otters were first reintroduced.

Never Give Up

Sea otters (*Enhydra lutris*) are the smallest marine mammal in North America and the second-largest member of the carnivorous family called Mustelidae. This means that sea otters' relatives include weasels, wolverines and badgers. There are 13 otter species, including the North American river otter, the neotropical otter, the giant otter and the African clawless otter. People in North America often confuse river otters with sea otters. Yet river otters are quite different from sea otters. They are much smaller than sea otters, they are long and slender with pointed tails, and they never swim on their backs. River otters also come ashore to den, and they eat their *prey* on land.

Three subspecies of sea otters are recognized: the Russian or Asian sea otter (found in the waters off the Commander Islands in the Bering Sea, the Kuril Islands in the western North Pacific Ocean and the northernmost Japanese islands), the northern sea otter (found from

This northern sea otter off the British Columbia coast is grooming itself. Sea otters have good reason to take care of their coats—they help them stay insulated in chilly waters.

Washington to Alaska) and the southern sea otter (found only in the waters off the California coast).

Having escaped extinction and recovered in different parts of their historical *range*, sea otters have demonstrated how special they are. They may be one of the most adorable creatures in the world, but there is much more to sea otters than cute, furry faces, and they constantly surprise those who observe them.

A SPECIES ON THE VERGE OF EXTINCTION

Most marine mammals, including whales and seals, rely on a layer of fat called blubber to keep them warm. Sea otters don't. Instead of blubber, they have a dense, water-resistant fur coat to insulate them from the frigid waters of the northern Pacific.

Sea otters have the thickest fur of any animal in the world—as many as one million hairs per square inch. (We humans have about 100,000 hairs on our heads.) The fur has two layers, an undercoat and a layer of long, waterproof guard hairs. This traps warm air next to the sea otter's skin. Sea otters spend a lot of time grooming and conditioning their fur to maintain that layer of insulating air. Even though sea otters live in water, their skin never gets wet.

While this special fur coat has protected sea otters against the cold for centuries, it also made them vulnerable to humans who wanted that fur for themselves. In 1741 an expedition led by explorer Vitus Bering came upon a sea-otter population in the Commander Islands off the eastern coast of Russia. The explorers went home with sea-otter pelts, and the luxurious sea-otter fur was soon in high demand throughout Russia, China, Japan and Europe.

A southern sea otter hauls out (comes ashore) on a sandy beach on the central coast of California.

A northern sea otter is resting on an iceberg in Alaska.
PETER NILE/GETTY IMAGES

For the next 160 years, ships and traders from North America, Russia, Britain and other countries hunted sea otters for their pelts, until the animals were almost wiped out. Nearly 15,000 sea otters per year were killed in the waters off Alaska at the turn of the 19th century.

Researchers don't know exactly how many sea otters existed prior to the fur trade but estimate between 100,000 and 300,000, with a range extending from the northern islands of Japan to Baja California, Mexico. Because sea otters were being hunted so intensely, Russia took measures to conserve the animals through a system of restrictions meant to sustain the population for continued hunting. Unfortunately, when Russia sold the territory of Alaska to the United States in 1867, those restrictions ended, and extreme hunting continued.

Sea-otter hunting was finally banned in 1911 by the International Fur Seal Treaty, but by then the sea otters were nearly gone. The Steller's sea cow, a marine mammal that the Bering expedition also encountered in 1741, had already been lost forever. An easily available source of meat, it had been hunted to extinction by 1768.

Luckily, sea otters as a species managed to survive human greed. Living in secret coves and sheltered reefs

The fur trade during the 18th and 19th centuries nearly drove sea otters to extinction by the early 1900s.
B-03051 ROYAL BC MUSEUM AND ARCHIVES

Sea otters often prefer shallow coastal waters.

Female sea otters usually spend their lives in one place and do not move much, but males venture out farther and explore larger areas.

on the rocky coast, 13 small remnant populations, totaling fewer than 2,000 animals, persisted in the North Pacific into the early 20th century. These tiny colonies were in isolated places, and they were almost all located near the northern limit of the sea-otter habitat, except for one single small colony on the coast of central California.

Back from the Brink

Since hunting was banned, sea otters are recolonizing their former habitats. In the 1960s people started becoming more aware of the need to conserve endangered species and repair the damage caused by humans. In the United States, sea otters received protection with the adoption of the Marine Mammal Protection Act in 1972 and the Endangered Species Act in 1973. Canada passed the Species at Risk Act in 2002.

Also in the 1960s, a number of sea-otter reintroduction programs were put in place to help sea-otter populations recover. Sea otters were reintroduced to British Columbia, southeast Alaska, Washington and Oregon. Today about 35 percent of the global sea-otter population can be attributed to those early translocations. The world population of sea otters is now estimated at about 125,000, living in locations along the coasts of central California, Washington, British Columbia, southeast Alaska, Prince William Sound, the Aleutian Islands and the Commander Islands.

In British Columbia the last sea otters were killed in 1929 and 1931 near the village of Kyuquot on Vancouver Island. Between 1969 and 1972, 89 sea otters were brought from Alaska to the west coast of Vancouver Island. An ecological reserve was created in 1981 to protect the

A raft of sea otters like this one serves as protection against attacks from predators.

sea-otter colony in Checleset Bay, where the animals were first reintroduced. Since then their numbers and range have expanded rapidly, and there are now nearly 7,000 of them along the west coast of Vancouver Island and the central coast of British Columbia.

In California, researchers believed that the fur trade had completely eliminated sea otters, estimated to have once numbered between 16,000 and 20,000. In the 1930s, approximately 50 sea otters were discovered off Big Sur in Monterey County, on the coast of central California. Since receiving protection, southern sea otters have gradually expanded to the north and the south along the central California coast. Today there are about 3,000 sea otters in the region.

IN THE FIELD:
How many can you see?

It's a sunny morning in early July, and I am on a small research boat with marine-mammal biologist Linda Nichol and her team from Fisheries and Oceans Canada. We are in Clayoquot Sound, on the west coast of Vancouver Island. As we travel, Linda meticulously scans the islets and reefs through binoculars. Her mission is to count all the sea otters she can find.

Only 20 minutes after leaving Tofino Harbour, she spots the first sea otter—a single male swimming off Vargas Island. She makes a note of the time and location. Despite her years of experience, Linda says the furry animals can be surprisingly hard to find. I understand why. It is easy to mistake their small, shiny heads on the surface of the water for harbor seals or even pieces of kelp. Sometimes they are impossible to see behind the waves, as both boats and sea otters rise and fall with the swell of the sea.

Linda looks forward to checking on the sea otters as if they were old friends, finding them in the places where they hang out and wondering how they have all fared over the winter. She now has many more friends to check on. Since she began counting sea otters in the early 2000s, their population in British Columbia has doubled. At the end of our day together, she has counted 144 sea otters. She has found many of them in **rafts**—the floating groups sea otters form in order to rest. Males and females float in separate rafts, which vary in size. Some rafts have more than 200 sea otters. Rafts usually form in the same locations, at a particular reef or kelp bed that the sea otters like.

Rafts of sea otters are difficult to approach and are easily disturbed by boat traffic.

Home Sweet Home

Because shallow waters offer feeding opportunities and protection from predators, sea otters tend to live in *nearshore* coastal habitats, often close to human activity. Most southern sea otters in California, for example, live within 1.2 miles (2 kilometers) of shore. Many of them feed and rest around the central coast's kelp forests, which give them some protection from strong waves. Sea otters often wrap themselves around pieces of kelp so they do not drift away while they sleep. Kelp forests are also a safe place for females to nurse and raise their pups.

Researchers have learned that female sea otters are very local—they live their lives in one place and do not move much. Scientists call this *site fidelity*. Female sea otters in particular tend to stay within the same 6- to 12-mile (10- to 20-kilometer) stretch of coastline. Males usually venture out farther and explore larger areas. Sea otters are a useful *indicator species* for humans, reflecting changes in environmental conditions. If sea otters are not doing well in an area, this may mean something is wrong with the overall health of the environment. The water may be contaminated, for example, which ultimately has a negative impact on us too.

A southern sea otter eating a clam in Elkhorn Slough, CA.

A VORACIOUS APPETITE

Sea otters love seafood, and they eat a lot of it. It's part of their unique body design. Their high metabolic rate helps them stay warm, and to fuel it they must eat 25 percent of their body weight in food every day. That means sea otters spend a lot of time—20 to 50 percent of their day—looking for food. By comparison, *carnivores* who live on

Female sea otters usually give birth to a single pup. The pups can be born at any time of the year. They stay with their mothers for the first eight months of their lives.

land eat 5 to 14 percent of their body weight per day and spend only 14 percent of their day hunting for prey.

Sea otters eat a wide range of marine *invertebrates*, including sea urchins, clams, abalone, crabs, mussels, sea cucumbers and on rare occasions even fish and seabirds. Scientists have reported that sea otters consume more than 150 different types of prey. But their favorite food is sea urchins. When sea otters first arrive in a rocky habitat, they eat all the urchins they can find, until they are all gone. Then they search for what else is on the seafloor menu.

These eating machines are efficient predators when it comes to finding food. They can dive as deep as 328 feet (100 meters), although they rarely do. Usually they look for *shellfish* in waters less than 131 feet (40 meters) deep. Once they find an urchin, clam or some other type of shellfish, they bring it back to the surface, float on their backs and use their stomachs as picnic tables.

Red, purple and green sea urchins in Haida Gwaii, BC.
LYNN LEE

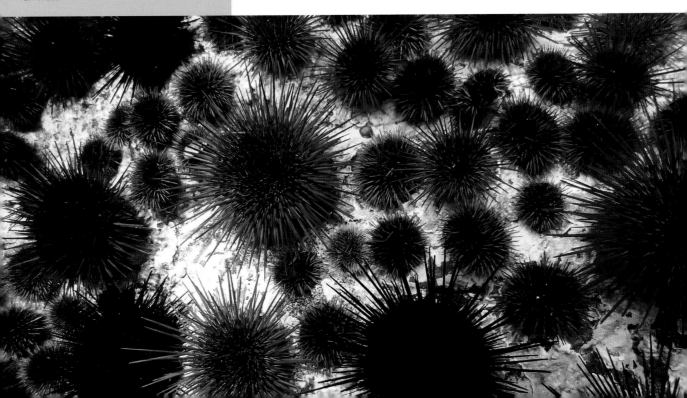

I once observed a lone male sea otter in the waters near the village of Kyuquot on Vancouver Island. The sea otter was busy hunting, and I watched him bring two large, bright-red crabs to the surface. He carefully laid the crabs on his stomach and started eating the first crab. I couldn't help feeling sorry for the other crab, who was the next item on the menu. In no time the sea otter was diving again, looking for more food.

Sea otters hunt in dark or murky water, so how do they actually locate dinner? They use their front paws to explore the underwater environment and their long, sensitive whiskers to detect the movement of their small prey.

Smash and Eat

Sea otters eat many invertebrates that are protected by hard shells. How do they avoid breaking their teeth when they bite into those thick shells? Sea otters have

Sea otters use their sense of touch and sensitive front paws to find food on the ocean floor.

Sea otters have strong teeth that allow them to crack into hard-shelled invertebrates.

tooth enamel that is much tougher than that of humans, and it contains additional layers of a protein-rich gel that works to prevent cracks from spreading (maybe this is useful information for dentists!).

But their bite force alone is not always sufficient to open the species with the heaviest armor, such as marine snails or clams. Sea otters are incredibly resourceful when it comes to food, and they have found the solution to spare their super teeth. They use tools. In fact, they are one of the few animals known to use tools. Others include primates, dolphins, and crows.

Sea otters find stones or empty shells and use them as hammers to crack open hard-shelled invertebrates. Because they have more snails in their diet, sea otters in California waters use tools more often than their northern counterparts do. Pups learn how from their mothers and refine their technique year after year, until they are able to crack even the toughest snails in no time. In places where they live near people, the ingenious sea otters have come up with new techniques. They pound shellfish against

This southern sea otter is using a rock as a tool to crack into a clam.

human-made structures, such as docks, jetties, boat hulls (which can be very annoying to a sleeping sailor) and ship ladders.

Sea otters often hold on to a favorite stone by tucking it under an armpit when diving and dropping it when it is no longer needed. They also use tools to knock prey off underwater rocks or pry it out of crevices.

Researchers can easily observe sea otters using tools because the animals return to the surface and float on their backs while processing their catch. Erin Foster, a research ecologist who has spent a lot of time studying what sea otters eat, remembers once seeing 50 male sea otters feeding over kelp beds after getting blown into a small cove during a winter storm on the central coast of British Columbia. The sea otters were pulling up red turban snails and smashing them in half on rocks. Erin remembers that all the rocks made slightly different sounds. There were so many sea otters eating, it was like being in a middle of a drumming circle.

BRINGING UP BABY

I love watching a sea-otter pup sleeping comfortably on its mom's tummy. It is always an adorable sight, and the babies look so relaxed. I sometimes complain about how much work it is to raise kids, but it's nothing compared to what female sea otters have to do. I have learned that they really are super moms. A female sea otter gives birth in the water to a single pup once a year. She floats on her back, holding the baby snugly on her chest to nurse it. The pup's fluffy, thick fur acts as a personal flotation device that keeps it from sinking underwater.

It takes about six months for a female sea otter to raise a pup until it is weaned and starting to feed itself. During that time, the pup is highly dependent on its mother for food.

Volunteers observe sea-otter behavior and contribute to a multiyear research project on the sea-otter population of Elkhorn Slough, CA.

Before the mom goes diving for food, she wraps her pup in kelp to stop it from drifting away and to hide it from predators that might come around while she is not there to protect it.

The pup floats on top of the water like a cork, cradled by kelp, waiting for its mother to return. Sea-otter pups suckle for five to eight months, until they are almost the size of an adult, and they need constant attention until they develop their survival skills. Moms share pieces of shellfish with babies and show the pups how to hunt.

In addition to producing milk, a mother has to spend time looking for food. A recent study of sea otters in California found that the daily energy demands on a female sea otter increase by 17 percent after she gives birth. After the pup is weaned, the demands on the mother are 96 percent higher than for a female without a pup.

Some females put so much energy into their pups that they can't recover afterward. It's similar to running out of gas. Sea-otter moms can become so weak and run-down that they are unable to survive the stress of a minor wound or infection. This is what scientists call *end-lactation syndrome*, which accounts for high mortality among female sea otters in some areas in California. A female sea otter is more likely to abandon her pup soon after it is born if she does not have enough energy reserves. This strategy helps ensure her own survival so that she can live to produce more pups in the future, rather than die trying to raise this current, single pup. Young females are more likely to adopt this strategy because they have the most reproductive potential to lose if they were to die when they raise their first or second pup.

As females age, their reproductive potential declines, so they seem to put more effort into their current pup's survival and are less likely to abandon their pup during the early stages. That means they push the limits in terms of how much energy they transfer to their growing pup. They become very emaciated themselves by the time the pup is old enough to wean. Sometimes the females can recover again after the pup weans, but sometimes they can't.

Sea-otter moms are truly some of the most devoted and hardworking mothers on the planet.

A female southern sea otter and her pup in California. Pups have high-pitched calls, which they use to communicate with their mothers.

IN THE FIELD:
Tell me what you eat

Watching Tim Tinker observe sea otters is intense. Tim, a wildlife biologist with the United States Geological Survey, has watched sea otters for 20 years—in Russia, Alaska, California and British Columbia. He has always been fascinated by the diet of sea otters and is able to identify what a sea otter is eating within seconds, right down to the exact size of the snail or clam it is handling.

Normally it can be difficult to observe what marine mammals do. After all, they spend a lot of their time underwater, out of sight. But sea otters live most of their lives at the surface and stay close to shore, which allows researchers to watch them through high-powered telescopes and learn about their day-to-day lives. Researchers can study the same animals year after year and watch the females have pups and raise them. They get to know individual personalities, and they can establish an *activity budget* that details everything a sea otter does through the day—resting, grooming, eating, foraging, traveling, socializing and so on. When sea otters die, they often end up on the beach, where scientists recover their carcasses to learn what killed them and, ultimately, how to better protect them.

I joined Tim and his team on a mission to capture sea otters in Monterey, California, as part of his long-term monitoring program in the region. Divers catch sea otters in humane traps and bring them to the Monterey Bay Aquarium, where a veterinary team takes a series of body measurements, obtains blood and fur samples and implants the animals with radio tracking devices. Some of the sea otters are also fitted with a time and depth recorder that measures how much time a sea otter spends diving and how deep it dives. The sea otters are then released back into the wild, and for years they are monitored daily by biologists and volunteers.

Through this program, scientists have gained extensive knowledge of the sea otters. Yet they are still surprised by how creative the sea otters are, how they adapt to their environment and, most of all, how they interact with other species and affect the ecosystem around them in so many different ways.

Wildlife biologist Tim Tinker and Dr. Mike Murray, director of veterinary services at the Monterey Bay Aquarium, give a checkup to a sea otter before it is released back into Monterey Bay, CA.

By controlling the size and number of sea
urchins, sea otters have created an opportunity
for kelp forests to grow and flourish.
ARCHIPELAGO WILDLIFE CRUISES

2

A Keystone Star Is Born

After being hunted almost to extinction, sea otters returned to old territories that had been without sea otters for more than a century, setting the stage for a fascinating natural experiment that profoundly changed the scientific understanding of how the natural world works. Scientists had a unique chance to witness an ecological revolution unfold right before their eyes.

A WORLD WITHOUT SEA OTTERS

When sea otters disappeared from their coastal habitats, sea urchins took over the undersea world. Because they weren't being eaten by hungry sea otters, the urchins increased in number and size. With urchins running the show, the marine landscape looked very different. Sea urchins are *herbivores* (plant eaters), and they love to eat algae, including kelp. They voraciously mowed down enormous amounts of the kelp growing on the rocky seafloor. Once the kelp was gone, the underwater rocky reefs became an *urchin barren*. In other words, urchins became the dominant species there.

Urchins were not the only lucky winners when sea otters disappeared. Other invertebrates thrived in the sea-otter-free environment. Abalone, Dungeness crabs and geoducks (a giant clam) all benefited from an easy and long life with no predators. They had a chance to become large and abundant.

As these invertebrates grew in size and number, humans saw new opportunities for themselves. They started collecting the invertebrates to sell all over the world and established commercial shellfish fisheries, which gave people jobs. When scuba-diving technology allowed fishermen to go underwater and collect invertebrates

An urchin barren in Haida Gwaii, BC.
LYNN LEE

from the seafloor, ancient urchins and geoducks were found. Undisturbed by sea otters, these species had lived to be more than 100 years old. The geoduck, which can bury itself more than three feet (one meter) deep in the gravel or sand of the ocean floor, is the largest and one of the longest-living burrowing clams in the world. In Canada, the oldest recorded geoduck was 168 years old. If sea otters had been around to eat them, geoducks certainly would not have had a chance to grow that old!

SEA OTTERS, KELP AND SEA URCHINS

For many years people in coastal areas considered the overabundance of shellfish normal. They could not imagine a different ecosystem. When sea otters returned to the rocky reef habitats, however, ecologists started noticing changes. Urchin barrens disappeared, and kelp forests started to grow. What was going on? Was it possible that the cute sea otters were responsible for the changes the ecologists were seeing?

Sea otters often wrap themselves in pieces of kelp so they don't drift away while they sleep.

Two traits of sea otters create the perfect recipe for ecological change. They have high site fidelity (which means they spend their entire lives in a small area), and, most important, they have a ferocious appetite and taste for those big sea urchins on the seafloor. So when sea otters arrive in an area for the first time, it seems like a tornado has hit the landscape. The sea otters get to work immediately. They look for their favorite food, the sea urchin.

What happens next looks like an action-packed film sequence and ecologists are still discovering the implications of the sea otters' appetite. Once the sea otters have devoured the sea urchins, the kelp forests start to grow again, since fewer urchins are there to eat them. And the growth is fast and furious. One study found that kelp forests were nearly 20 times larger on the west coast of Vancouver Island where sea otters had eliminated the red sea urchins.

Ecologists started to see a clear link between sea otters and kelp. They found sea otters had a lot more to offer than their cuteness. Their ability to keep urchins from growing too abundant benefited the entire ecosystem. With their great ecological powers, sea otters became the best-known example of what scientists call a *keystone species*.

A purple sea urchin climbing up
to graze on bull kelp in an urchin
barren in Haida Gwaii, BC.
LYNN LEE

An ochre sea star (also known as the purple sea star) at low tide in British Columbia. Like the sea otter, the purple sea star is considered a keystone species.

A marine ecologist named Bob Paine came up with that term, but he didn't have sea otters in mind when he did. *Keystone* is an architectural term for the small, wedge-shaped stone at the top of an arch that keeps the arch from collapsing. When it comes to wildlife, a keystone species is one that has the power to hold an ecosystem together in the same way a keystone prevents an arch from collapsing.

In the 1960s Bob demonstrated the concept of a keystone species by conducting an experiment with purple sea stars along the rocky coast of Washington State. At low tide he removed all the sea stars from a stretch of shoreline. Within two years California mussels had started to monopolize this stretch. By contrast, the areas where sea stars were left undisturbed had many different species—anemones, sponges, mussels, barnacles, chitons, limpets and various types of seaweeds.

What happened? Sea stars love to eat mussels, so when sea stars are removed from an area, the mussels no longer have a predator and can expand freely. In fact, mussels are so aggressive that they take over all the space. Other species have a hard time competing and exist only in very small numbers. Through this simple experiment, Bob discovered that one keystone species, the purple sea star, had a huge influence on its environment. Its position in the *food chain* proved to be crucial in maintaining the biodiversity of an entire area.

It was another scientist who connected sea otters to the keystone concept. In the 1970s a young ecologist named Jim Estes traveled to the Aleutian Islands in Alaska to study sea otters. The fur trade there had set the stage for a perfect natural experiment. Jim compared

two islands: Amchitka, where sea otters were abundant, and Shemya, where sea otters had been entirely wiped out by the fur trade. Jim methodically surveyed the seafloor at each site. Diving in all seasons, he counted urchins and measured the kelp. At Amchitka, where the sea otters had survived, Jim dove into a lush, thick kelp forest. He found that many species lived and fed in the kelp, from small invertebrates to fish and seals. There were few urchins. At Shemya, where there were no sea otters, Jim found himself in what looked like a clear-cut landscape, with lots of huge urchins on the seafloor and hardly any kelp in sight.

As Jim moved between these two strikingly different environments, the story became clear. The only difference between the sites was the sea otter. Jim had just discovered that the urchin-munching sea otters ruled the undersea world, holding the true power of a keystone species. Even though people already knew that sea otters ate urchins and urchins ate kelp, Jim was the first to connect the dots. Who would have thought that the sea otters were capable of making such a big difference?

Green sea urchins grazing on kelp on the central coast of British Columbia.
LYNN LEE

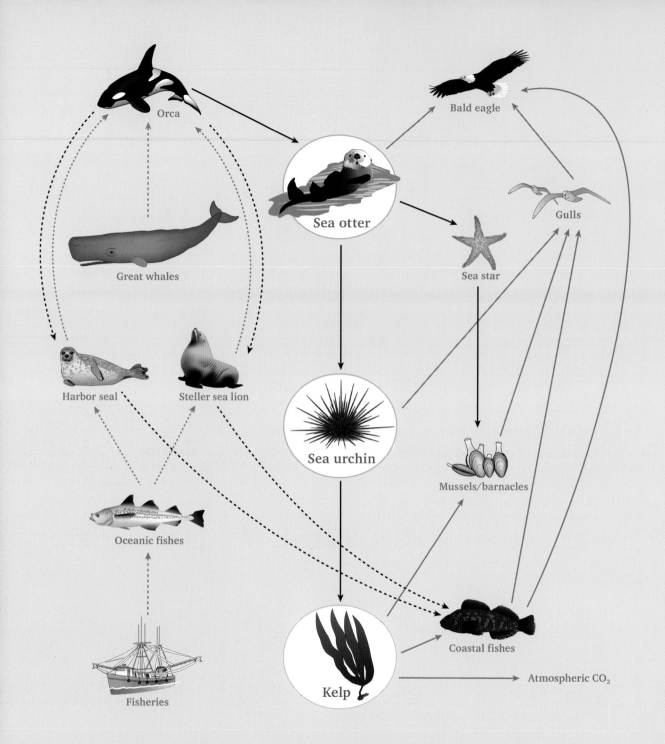

This diagram outlines how complex the ecological influence of sea otters can be. Black arrows show top-down links, or how sea otters and other animals can affect their prey. The gray arrows show bottom-up links, or how species can affect the animals that graze or prey upon them. Effects that are well documented are shown by solid arrows. Effects that are not as well known are shown as dashed arrows. ADAPTED FROM JAMES A. ESTES ET AL. "MEGAFAUNAL IMPACTS ON STRUCTURE AND FUNCTION OF OCEAN ECOSYSTEMS," *ANNU. REV. ENVIRON. RESOUR.* (2016) 41:83–116. DOI.ORG/10.1146/ANNUREV-ENVIRON-110615-085622

The sea otters were the starting point of an unbelievable chain reaction that transformed the ecosystem around them. This process is an example of a *trophic cascade*, a domino effect whereby a predator at the top of the food chain can change an ecosystem through its impacts on prey. The gray wolf provides another example of a trophic cascade involving a predator. When wolves were reintroduced to Yellowstone National Park in the 1990s after many years of absence, they hunted elk. As a result, the elk population decreased. With fewer elk grazing on plants, species such as aspen started recovering, and the entire ecosystem became more vegetated, which created habitats for other important species.

Jim's discovery revealed an important conservation lesson. When humans hunted sea otters to near extinction, they eliminated the critical role of a key predator, disrupting a fundamental trophic cascade that shaped the natural world—and they had no idea what they had done.

Sea otters are suited to an aquatic life. They have nostrils and ears that close in the water, their feet are webbed to make swimming easier and their tails are flatter at the end to go faster underwater.

IN THE FIELD:
Diving in sea-otter country

Jane Watson grew up on the coast of British Columbia and knew from an early age that she wanted to be a marine biologist. For over 30 years she has been diving on the west coast of Vancouver Island, chronicling the impacts of the sea otters' return. Just as Jim Estes studied sea otters in the Aleutian Islands, Jane saw a scientific opportunity with the sea-otter reintroduction and the animals' gradual expansion in British Columbia to learn more about their effect on the shallow, rocky environment. She chose specific sites, a mix of areas where sea otters had been established the longest, areas they were moving into and areas where they were still absent, and every summer she returned to survey those exact locations. In 30 years she never missed a field season.

Jane has spent more than 6,000 hours underwater. She was one of the first scientists in British Columbia to witness an extraordinary underwater revolution in natural history: urchin barrens transforming into beautiful forests of giant kelp.

Jane describes her exploration of urchin barrens as floating in a pink world, created by the overwhelming abundance of pink coralline algae. Invertebrates such as sea urchins, abalone, chitons and sea cucumbers are all easy to see, thriving in the open. Diving in this landscape is like walking in a grassland, where everything is exposed. In stark contrast, diving in the rich brown kelp is like hiking in an old-growth forest with light streaming through the canopy. The difference is the kelp forest is teeming with fish instead of birds and land animals.

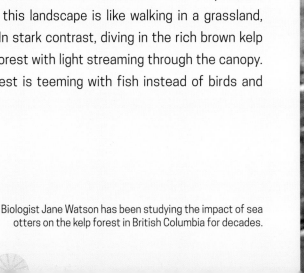

Biologist Jane Watson has been studying the impact of sea otters on the kelp forest in British Columbia for decades.

IN THE FIELD:
In the underwater forest

In British Columbia, Jane Watson has observed what happens when sea otters come into an area. Once they eat the urchins, kelp plants start to grow, and this can happen really quickly. Sometimes it takes just a few months to grow a kelp forest again. When sea otters remove urchins, the first species of kelp that appears is usually the bull kelp (*Nereocystis luetkeana*), a seaweed that lives for only a year and grows up to 39 feet (12 meters) long. It consists of a long stipe (or stalk) attached to the ocean floor by a **holdfast** of many fingerlike projections. It appears at the ocean surface as a single float from which a cluster of blades arise.

The following year, the bull kelp is sometimes replaced by a perennial (living for more than one year) kelp species (*Pterygophora californica*) that grows to about 6.5 feet (2 meters) tall and can live for up to 25 years. This plant has several names. Watson calls it old-growth kelp or tree kelp. Indigenous Peoples call it walking kelp, because when it attaches to large rocks it moves around in shallow waters. They collected the plant and used it to direct salmon into their fish traps. In areas more sheltered from waves, another species, called giant kelp (*Macrocystis pyrifera*), can grow to 98 feet (30 meters) long. Giant kelp forms a canopy, shading the underwater forest below and providing habitat to myriad species.

The age of the old-growth kelp can be determined by examining its growth rings, just as with trees. By counting the rings, Jane was able to determine when the sea otters arrived in a particular area.

When the old-growth kelp reaches maturity—17 to 20 years in British Columbia—the plants fall down, and the whole underwater kelp forest transforms. The process starts all over again and new kelp grows—and not always in a predictable manner. Her long-term studies have allowed Jane to witness this process repeat itself, with all the wonderful variations and surprises that the natural world offers.

A bull kelp forest in Haida Gwaii, BC.
LYNN LEE

When kelp dies and washes up on beaches, it provides food and habitat for animals that live on land.

THE WEALTH OF KELP FORESTS

Sea otters revive kelp forests, but is it a reason to celebrate? Why should we care about kelp?

It turns out that kelp forests are among the most productive ecosystems in the world, full of rich marine life. Their diversity and exuberance can be compared to those of a rainforest. A thriving kelp forest is a safe haven and food source for many species of fish, as well as thousands of invertebrates. A study led by biologist David Duggins found that mussels and barnacles in the Aleutian Islands were enriched by kelp-derived carbon and grew two to three times faster at islands where sea otters were present than at those where sea otters were not. Another study found that Alaskan kelp forests with healthy sea-otter populations had up to 10 times more rock greenling, a type of fish.

Kelp forests are active nurseries for many young fish, who can hide in them to evade predators. Kelp forests also slow down water flow, which ensures that the larvae of a variety of marine fishes and invertebrates such as abalone can stay and grow in the kelp rather than be swept away by currents. Kelp is also as useful dead as alive. The forest is constantly shedding pieces of kelp, and these dead parts fall onto the seafloor or into crevices, where they are picked up and eaten by organisms such as abalone, snails and urchins.

The benefits of kelp are felt all the way up the food chain. Kelp attracts large marine mammals such as seals, sea lions and orcas, who use kelp forests as hunting grounds. Russell Markel was the first biologist to estimate how much deeper and larger kelp grows in British Columbia when sea otters are present. He remembers swimming to

A copper rockfish in the kelp forests on the west coast of Vancouver Island, BC. LYNN LEE

the surface after a dive near Kyuquot and spotting three mammal-eating transient orcas hunting at the edge of the huge kelp forest. Two animals were patrolling the outside of the forest while one dived into the kelp to catch a harbor seal—one of orcas' favorite foods. The orcas knew harbor seals would be hunting the abundant fish in the kelp forest.

Healthy kelp forests nourish numerous species, including humans. Archaeologists hypothesize that kelp forests were once an important "marine highway" for Indigenous Peoples in North America. Boats were easier to navigate on these highways, as the forests reduced wave action. As breakwaters, kelp beds also help reduce the erosion of shorelines.

Bald eagles usually build their nests with tree branches, but a researcher has discovered eagles also use kelp as nesting material.

Their positive impact on kelp means that sea otters may be able to help with the biggest environmental challenge of our times—climate change. The larger kelp forests found where sea otters are present have the capacity, through photosynthesis, to capture billions of pounds of *carbon dioxide* from the atmosphere.

A Kelp Nest for Bald Eagles

During walks on the beaches of the west coast of British Columbia, I often come across translucent brown kelp stipes. My children sometimes pick them up for the shell and driftwood houses they build in hopes that crabs and other animals will use them as homes.

Kelp does not just nourish myriad species in the ocean. When it dies and washes up on the beach, it continues to support life. Beach-cast kelp provides food and habitat to animals that live in the *intertidal zone* and on land, including birds and small mammals. Sometimes kelp is used in unexpected ways.

While she was studying sea otters in Gosling Rocks on British Columbia's central coast, ecologist Erin Foster discovered an eagle nest on top of a spruce tree that stood 8.2 feet (2.5 meters) high. The nest was made of dried,

This bald eagle nest was built with pieces of old-growth kelp (*Pterygophora californica*).
ERIN FOSTER

woody pieces of old-growth kelp that the eagles had picked up from the shore. Erin was surprised, as eagle nests are usually constructed with wood from tree branches.

Gosling Rocks is an isolated group of about 70 rocky islets. Only one islet is treed. Eagles had to make repeated trips to the nearest forested area, which is almost two miles (three kilometers) away, in order to find branches for their nest.

But with the return of the sea otters and the revival of the kelp forest, the birds no longer have to make that long trek. They discovered they can use kelp stipes for their nests rather than branches from the more distant treed area. Access to this new construction material saves the birds time and energy, making their lives easier. The eagles also benefit from the sea otters' return because there is more fish in the kelp forest for them to eat.

It's another example of how sea otters influence life in diverse ways, not just in the sea but also on land.

Bald eagles and sea otters are connected in surprising ways.

When sea otters return to an area, they help create healthy kelp forests. Kelp in turn supports many species that live in the ocean and on land.

IN THE FIELD:
Understanding the small things

When they want to understand sea otters' influence on a local ecosystem, researchers methodically survey specific underwater areas, counting and measuring everything they see. It is not easy to get a full picture of all the species that live in a kelp forest. Some animals are tiny, and others are too difficult to sample in the field. To address this problem, biologists scrape a small area of the seafloor and collect everything they can find with an air-powered underwater vacuum. This process takes a team of two divers. One diver dislodges the animals, and the other diver vacuums them into a nylon sample bag. The nylon bag is sealed and tagged. Larger invertebrates are identified, weighed and returned to the field, and the remaining invertebrates are stored and identified later in the laboratory. Seaweeds are also identified and weighed, and specimens are mounted on herbarium paper (a herbarium is a collection of dried plant specimens) and kept for reference.

In the different areas where sea otters live, marine scientists need to know what happens in the sea otters' underwater world. They rely on scuba-diving surveys to understand the complex relationships between sea otters and their environment.

Researchers Dan Malone and Shannon Myers from the University of California, Santa Cruz examine a piece of giant kelp after a dive survey to understand the complex relationship between kelp forests, sea otters, sea urchins and other invertebrates in Monterey Bay, CA.

Black oystercatchers love to eat mussels. They use their long bills to open them.

A Meal for Oystercatchers

I love black oystercatchers. With their loud, high-pitched whistles and their long, bright bills, they are one of my favorite shorebirds. I love to watch them when I walk on rocky shorelines. Once when I was kayaking near Kyuquot, I noticed a significant number of oystercatchers on the rocks. I was surprised to see so many. I was in the heart of sea-otter country, the first area to which sea otters had been reintroduced 50 years earlier. Did sea otters have something to do with oystercatchers being so abundant here?

Local researchers were curious about this too. They discovered there were more oystercatchers in this area, where the sea otters had been reestablished the longest, than there were in places where sea otters had arrived more recently. Why? One idea that might explain this increase is the interaction between oystercatchers, sea otters and mussels. Oystercatchers love mussels and limpets, and these birds patrol the intertidal habitat feeding on both, using their long bills to pry mussels open and pull limpets off the rocks. Sea otters love mussels too. They pull bunches of large mussels off the rocks in the intertidal zone, leaving bare patches on the rocks for limpets and young mussels to settle and grow, which may be easier for oystercatchers to catch.

A Meal for Wolves

Directly and indirectly, sea otters support all sorts of animals, from small invertebrates to big animals such as wolves—which sometimes means a sad ending for the sea otters. In British Columbia, elusive coastal wolves move quietly along the shorelines of Vancouver Island, searching for their next meal. They swim from island to island, relying entirely on the food the ocean provides—salmon, barnacles, clams and herring eggs. Expert beachcombers, the wolves even feast on whales that wash up dead on the shore. As much as 90 percent of a coastal wolf's diet comes from the sea.

They eat whatever comes their way—even sea otters. During a trip to a remote island off Vancouver Island, our guide discovered wolf poop that contained sea-otter fur

Coastal wolves spend much of their time on beaches in search of food.

A young visitor to a remote island off Vancouver Island holds a sea-otter skull that was found in the forest—possible evidence of a coastal wolf having eaten a sea otter for dinner.

and bone fragments. We realized that wolves sometimes scavenged for dead sea otters or even occasionally preyed on sea otters that had hauled out briefly on land. I felt sorry for the sea otters, but I was grateful for the magical experience of hearing, for the first time, wolves howling at night in the nearby forest.

A Lucky Duck

I love picnics on the beach in the summer, but sometimes we have uninvited guests—gulls. They watch every move we make in hopes of getting first dibs on any food we drop. I have watched gulls do the same thing with resident sea otters, shadowing them and grabbing any shellfish scraps they can get. These gulls are brave, because even though sea otters look adorable, they can be fierce, and they sometimes eat seabirds.

Gulls are not the only ones scooping up the leftovers. In February 2014, for the first time, researchers on the central coast of British Columbia observed harlequin ducks following sea otters in the winter. Sea otters dive down to collect red sea urchins from the seafloor. When they bring their catch to the surface, they leave uneaten fragments there, and the ducks feast on these leftovers. The sea urchins are too large and live too deep in the water for these shallow-diving ducks to access them, so whatever the sea otters leave behind is a real treat for the ducks. Urchins are highly nutritious, which is just what the ducks need to get through the winter and ready themselves for migrating in the spring to the freshwater streams near where they will nest. Harlequin ducks are smart, and they were observed following sea otters only in places the sea otters had recently come to, where urchins were a high proportion of the sea otters' diet.

Harlequin ducks follow sea otters to eat the floating sea-urchin bits that sea otters leave behind.

A gull tries to get scraps of leftover food from a southern sea otter in Elkhorn Slough, CA.

A southern sea otter floats
on its back in Elkhorn Slough, CA.
About 100 sea otters live in the estuary.

3

Unexpected Homes, Surprising Friends

The sea otter's recovery from the brink of extinction has proven to be much more than simply saving an adorable species. When sea otters returned and helped kelp forests grow and expand, they revived an entire ecosystem and all the species that depended on it. But their impact does not stop there. To people who pay attention, sea otters tell a story of ancient times, of how the natural world used to be.

AT HOME IN AN ESTUARY

In the 1980s a few sea otters started turning up in Elkhorn Slough, a major tidal *estuary* in Monterey Bay, on California's central coast. Elkhorn Slough provides habitat for a diverse range of birds, plants, marine mammals and fish. Harbor seals and California sea lions live there, and more than 340 species of birds have been identified in and around the slough.

At first researchers were surprised to find sea otters there and thought they would not stay long. The few sea otters that had survived the fur trade in California were found exclusively on the coast, so researchers just assumed they had stayed there, foraging in kelp beds.

When Lilian Carswell, a biologist with the US Fish and Wildlife Service, first noticed that sea otters were in Elkhorn Slough, she did not think the estuary could provide them with everything they needed to survive. She and other biologists thought the sea otters might be visiting the slough just to rest and would run out of food quickly.

But the sea otters proved everybody wrong. About 100 sea otters now reside in the estuary and are doing well. Field research has confirmed that some of the female sea otters spend their entire lives in the slough, which provides

Healthy seagrass beds support much of Elkhorn Slough's wildlife, including sea otters and harbor seals that share the habitat.

Elkhorn Slough provides habitat and shelter to hundreds of birds, fish, plants and marine mammals.

enough shellfish to eat to keep them going. Sea otters that live in the estuary spend less time looking for food, and because they do not have to dive as deep to find it—less than 10 feet (3 meters)—they also spend less energy catching it. What's more, living in Elkhorn Slough protects them from shark attacks, which are a leading cause of sea-otter death in California.

Elkhorn Slough is the first estuary in California that sea otters have inhabited in recent years. But historical and archaeological records indicate that a large number of sea otters once lived in estuaries. Adele Ogden's 1941 book *The California Sea Otter Trade, 1784–1848* notes that San Francisco Bay had numerous sea otters. But modern-day scientists had not seen sea otters in estuaries. The fur trade had eliminated sea otters from these habitats long before ecology as a science emerged in the last half of the 20th century, so researchers had no direct knowledge of all the places sea otters had inhabited in the past.

The fact that sea otters are now able to live in estuaries such as Elkhorn Slough has forced scientists to reconsider what they thought they knew about these creatures. They have learned there is much they still do not know about sea otters and predator species in general. It's as if humans, after nearly eliminating sea otters, forgot who they were, where they were and how they lived. It's similar to how we forget the family stories we heard from our parents about how their grandparents lived. Over time these stories become vague and more difficult to access—we tend to forget what life used to be like when nobody is around to tell us about it anymore.

The Sea Otter, the Crab and the Sea Slug

Elkhorn Slough is covered in salt marshes and seagrass beds. Seagrasses are flowering plants that have adapted to live in the marine environment. They form seagrass meadows, which are important ecosystems. They provide nursery habitat for young fish and invertebrates, and they protect shorelines from storms and waves. They control erosion by holding down and trapping *sediment*. Like kelp, seagrass absorbs carbon from the atmosphere and buries it in its roots, acting as a *carbon sink* (an area that accumulates and stores carbon), which is important for combating climate change. Unfortunately, seagrass meadows everywhere are declining because of human development and pollution.

Elkhorn Slough was no exception. It is located near the Salinas Valley, an area that produces a lot of fruits and vegetables. When farmers spray their crops with fertilizers, large quantities of polluted runoff end up in the slough. An excess of *nutrients* in the runoff spurs the growth of algae on seagrass leaves, which kills the seagrass plants because it blocks the sunlight they need. For a long time the seagrass beds of Elkhorn Slough were in trouble, just as many other estuaries were.

Sea otters promote the recovery of seagrass beds in Elkhorn Slough.

Sea otters often use their long, sensitive whiskers to detect the movements of their prey.

Marine biologist Brent Hughes inspects a seagrass blade in Elkhorn Slough.

But then something happened. Sea otters moved into the slough, and things started to change. Researchers noticed how healthy and green some of the seagrass beds in the slough had become. This surprised them, as the nutrient levels were still high. How could seagrass survive and expand in this highly polluted estuary? It did not make sense.

In 2010 marine biologist Brent Hughes set out to solve the mystery. Like a detective, he conducted an investigation. He reviewed all the data he could find, going back 50 years. He discovered that the presence of the sea otters was a crucial factor. The seagrass beds' recovery coincided with the sea otters' arrival at the slough.

But if sea otters helped the seagrass, how did they work their magic? Brent found a remarkable chain reaction leading to the seagrass comeback. When the sea otters returned to the slough, they put their big appetites to work, eating many crabs, favoring the large ones.

With fewer crabs to prey on them, grazing invertebrates—including a sea slug called the California sea hare—grew larger and more abundant. The sea hares fed on the harmful algae growing on the seagrass, leaving the leaves healthy and clean.

Brent conducted field experiments that simulated the sea otters' impacts on the local ecosystem, using enclosures in Elkhorn Slough. One of the enclosures contained the large crabs one would expect to find when sea otters are not around to eat them. The other had the smaller crabs found when sea otters are present. As expected, the seagrass grew larger and faster in the enclosure with the smaller crabs.

Researchers already knew about the three-level trophic cascade that involved sea otters, sea urchins and kelp. Now, in Elkhorn Slough, Brent had discovered a four-level trophic cascade—from sea otters to crabs to algae-grazing sea slugs to seagrass. This trophic cascade had made the seagrass beds the healthiest of any estuary he had seen on the west coast.

The discovery identified an entirely new keystone role for sea otters in estuaries. When sea otters settled in Elkhorn Slough, the move was good not just for them but also for an entire ecosystem. Many other estuaries in California are polluted, degraded and in need of help. People work hard to try to restore these important and fragile ecosystems. Perhaps what is needed is a little help from the ecology wizards sea otters have proven themselves to be. As they expand to other estuaries, they can restore the ecological web and help repair the damage done by humans. Sea otters give conservationists the hope that some of the things we've lost can be restored.

The sea otters' voracious appetites affect ecosystems in ways that scientists are just beginning to fully understand.

IN THE FIELD:
A beautiful sea hare

When I jumped into a boat in Elkhorn Slough with Brent Hughes to learn more about the impact of sea otters on seagrass, I finally got to meet the species he had fallen in love with. No one in the slough could take their eyes off the sea otters poking their heads out of the water—except Brent. His gaze was set on something else. He pulled a seagrass blade out of the water and showed me a sea hare (a large sea slug) on the blade. For a moment I admired the delicate green translucence of the slug. It was beautiful. But it was so much more. The seagrass and the slug belonged to each other. With the help of sea otters, the hares were fighting the harmful effects of nutrient pollution on seagrass. It was a real team effort to maintain the health of this ecosystem.

A California sea hare on seagrass in Elkhorn Slough.

A sea otter carries her pup in the seagrass of Elkhorn Slough. At birth, a newborn sea otter's coat, called a *lanugo*, acts like a life preserver and keeps the baby floating at the water's surface.

Seagrass beds provide a nursery habitat for young fish and invertebrates, and protect shorelines from storms and waves.

SEA OTTERS AND SEAGRASS

Now that they have discovered the positive impact sea otters have on nutrient-polluted seagrass in Elkhorn Slough, scientists wonder if sea otters can help seagrass beds in regions with different challenges.

In southeast Alaska, University of Alaska marine ecologist Ginny Eckert and her colleagues are trying to answer this question. Like researchers in California, they have observed that where there are sea otters, there are healthy, lush seagrass beds, although they do not yet completely understand why.

In British Columbia, too, the long-term influence of the furry ecosystem engineers on seagrass is still not fully understood. One theory is that when sea otters dig in the beds to find clams to eat, leaving foraging holes behind, they may be oxygenating the soil and helping the seagrass grow faster. Researchers Erin Foster and Jane Watson wonder if by disturbing seagrass beds, sea otters may help increase the genetic diversity of seagrass, which in turn makes seagrass beds stronger and more resilient.

In Elkhorn Slough sea otters helped to make the salt marsh ecosystem stronger.

SALT MARSH IN TROUBLE

Sea otters did not rescue just the seagrass in Elkhorn Slough. There is also a fragile salt-marsh habitat there, and scientists are discovering that sea otters are beneficial to this ecosystem too. Again, the story starts with the sea otters' insatiable appetite. Numerous striped shore crabs had made their home in the muddy banks of the estuary's salt marsh. As they burrowed into the banks and fed on the marsh roots, they created many holes. The banks looked like Swiss cheese, and they became so weak that they started crumbling. Salt-marsh erosion is common, occurring worldwide. Ninety-three percent of marshes on the Pacific coast of the United States have disappeared since European settlement.

In Elkhorn Slough, sea otters came to the rescue. They were first seen moving into the salt marsh of the slough in 2012. Almost as soon as they arrived, the marsh improved. The sea otters started eating the striped shore crabs. With fewer burrowing crabs, there were not as many holes as before. The muddy banks got stronger, and the marsh plants became more productive. Through their appetite for crab, the sea otters helped make the salt marsh healthier, slowed down erosion and increased shoreline stability.

Brent Hughes checks the enclosures he set in the salt marsh to conduct field experiments and understand the sea otters' impact on the local ecosystem.

IN THE FIELD:
Citizen science at work

Ron Eby, a retired navy officer who grew up on the east coast of the United States, loves being on the water. Since 2007 he has dedicated himself to watching sea otters in Elkhorn Slough, and he does it every single day along with other committed volunteers. Their observations have helped scientists understand where sea otters are, what they are doing and what role they play in the estuary. For example, Ron and his sea otter monitoring partner Robert Scoles saw sea otters hauling themselves out onto the shores of the salt marsh, which was a surprising behavior. While sea otters haul out on rocks in other locations, such as Alaska, this was the first time anyone had documented them hauling out in a salt marsh. When they get out of the water and onto land, sea otters get a chance to rest, conserve energy and warm up, as long as the spots where they haul out are quiet and away from people who might disturb them.

Ron Eby monitors sea otters in Elkhorn Slough.

ALONE MENU

BALONE SOLD LIVE IN SHELL

"QUARTER POUNDER"
$24 PER POUND

OLD

"THIRD POUNDER"
$25 PER POUND

R OLD

"HALF POUNDER"
$26 PER POUND

AR OLD

"THREE QUARTER POUNDER"
$27 PER POUND

EAR OLD

"ONE POUND"

Trevor Fay grows red abalone in Monterey, CA.

ABALONE'S BEST FRIEND?

When sea otters return, it's not good news for all species, particularly for the invertebrates that sea otters like to eat. One of the species sea otters eat is abalone, a large marine snail that is related to oysters and clams. In British Columbia, northern abalone is listed as "endangered," and so is black abalone in California. Both of these species were almost driven to extinction because of overfishing. In British Columbia, an intensive commercial dive fishery from the 1960s to the 1980s dramatically reduced the population of northern abalone, leading to the closure of all abalone fisheries in 1990.

Although we know that sea otters eat abalone, researchers have proved that they did not drive abalone to near extinction. Rather, sea otters influence abalone abundance, size and behavior. For example, abalone adopt a new lifestyle in order to live with their sea-otter neighbors.

Volunteer divers with the nonprofit group Reef Check monitor and remove purple sea urchins in an effort to restore the giant kelp forest in Monterey Bay, CA.

When there are no sea otters around to eat them, abalone grow large and settle in open, shallow waters, competing with urchins for rare kelp food.

When sea otters are present, the numbers of abalone are often reduced, and the remaining abalone try to avoid predation by moving deeper and hiding in crevices. Over time the abalone even get thinner to fit into narrow cracks. This allows them to stay safe from the paws of sea otters trying to catch them. In California, a study led by Peter Raimondi showed that black abalone occurred at higher densities in the places where sea otters had been present the longest and were most abundant. How could it be possible? Why would there be more abalone in areas where their most dangerous predator was also present?

One possible explanation for this unexpected result is that as sea otters eat urchins and promote kelp growth, they indirectly provide more food for the abalone that eat kelp. Where there are no sea otters around, urchins become more abundant and devour kelp. With little kelp around, abalone spend more time in the open, looking for food. In contrast, when sea otters are present, kelp forests flourish, and abalone can easily obtain food from drift kelp without moving from their safe hiding spots. They can remain in crevices, well fed and protected at the same time.

Sea otters also offer indirect protection to abalone against an even more dangerous predator: humans. Because abalone move to and hide in refuges that are difficult for sea otters to access—deep, narrow cracks and crevices—they also avoid the fishermen who try to poach them illegally.

In British Columbia, biologist Lynn Lee studied the interactions between sea otters and northern abalone and found that while sea otters directly reduced the number of abalone, they actually did not push the species to near extinction. As in California, abalone escaped sea-otter predation by hiding in crevices in deeper waters.

It turns out that sea otters and abalone are not enemies. They have always lived together. Now that sea otters are present in the ecosystem, however, abalone exist in a way that no longer works for fishermen. It is too difficult for people to harvest the well-hidden invertebrates, and the abalone are too small for commercial harvests. It is now the fishermen's turn to adapt, and adaptation is not always easy.

SEA OTTERS AND SEA STARS

Any popular movie relies on its stars, but the supporting cast is also important to tell the story. When you watch a movie like *The Incredibles*, you realize that superheroes cannot always save the world on their own. They need help, so they work in a team whose members have different powers that serve a common goal.

It works the same way in the kelp forest. We know that sea otters are the stars of the ecosystem. Their ecological

Red sea urchins and ochre sea stars exposed at low tide in the intertidal zone in Haida Gwaii, BC. LYNN LEE

power is acknowledged and celebrated. But sometimes they just cannot be incredible all by themselves, and scientists have discovered an important supporting character in the kelp forest that they had not really noticed until recently.

Jenn Burt, a marine ecologist at Simon Fraser University in Vancouver, was interested in learning more about how the rocky reefs changed as sea-otter populations expanded on the central coast of British Columbia. She chose 11 study sites, a mix of areas with well-established sea-otter populations, areas with no sea otters and areas where sea otters had recently arrived. In 2013 she started conducting underwater surveys to monitor the changes. She was already well aware that sea otters keep the kelp forest healthy by eating sea urchins.

Two years after she started her work, a surprising event happened to the sunflower sea star, one of the largest sea stars in the world. In 2015 and 2016, sea star wasting disease killed 96 percent of the sunflower sea stars on British Columbia's central coast.

But why would having less sea stars affect kelp forests? It turned out that sea otters were not the only ones keeping the kelp-forest ecosystem together. They had been getting help from a partner, the sunflower sea star, but people did not appreciate how important this connection was until the stars were completely gone from the ecosystem. Because Jenn started to monitor the habitat two years before the sea stars were wiped out and continued monitoring for two years after, she was able to witness and compare the changes.

How did sea otters and sea stars work together? Sea otters can be picky eaters. They choose to eat the larger,

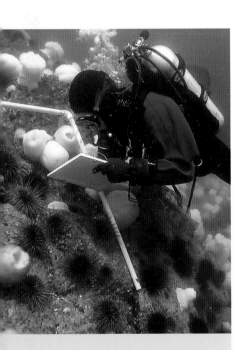
A diver conducts a rocky reef survey.
JENN BURT

This kelp forest in Monterey, CA, provides habitats for invertebrates such as anemones and fish species such as blue rockfish.
JOE TOMOLEONI

In an effort to understand how sea otters are responding to the proliferation of sea urchins in Monterey Bay after the loss of sea stars, wildlife biologist Tim Tinker and his team are attaching radio tracking devices to sea otters. Once the sea otters are released back to the wild, researchers can follow their movements and learn what effects they are having on the local ecosystem.

more nutritious sea urchins and do not bother about the smaller ones. This is where the sunflower sea star comes in. Sea stars cannot eat large urchins because of their long spines, so instead they eat the small and medium-sized urchins that the sea otters ignore and clean up what the sea otters leave behind. In doing so they play an important role in maintaining the health of the kelp forest. Jenn observed that kelp density was highest at reefs with both sea otters and sunflower stars. Without the sunflower stars, the delicate balance of the kelp-forest ecosystem was disrupted. Without the sea stars to eat them, the smaller urchins proliferated and ate the kelp, which suffered as a result. During this period there was a 311 percent increase in small and medium-sized sea urchins, which corresponded to a 30 percent decrease in kelp density.

When kelp is abundant, sea urchins usually live in crevices and cracks, where they can stay hidden and eat pieces of kelp that drift by. But when urchin predators are not around and kelp is in short supply, urchins come out of their hiding spots and actively roam for kelp to munch on. In northern California—where sea otters are not present—the combination of a "sea urchin boom" following the sea-star die-off, and an El Niño event that brought nutrient-poor warm waters to the coast, created a very stressful situation for kelp. In just a few years the kelp forest declined by over 80 percent in this region.

Farther south on the central California coast, near Monterey, researchers also witnessed urchin outbreaks—a tenfold increase in the number of urchins in 2014. They did not expect to see so many urchins appear in sea-otter country. Why weren't the sea otters doing their job and protecting the kelp from the urchins?

The veterinary team at the Monterey Bay Aquarium examines a sea otter that has just been implanted with a tracking device for a long-term monitoring project.

Ecologist Joshua Smith holds a purple sea urchin at the University of California, Santa Cruz. He is studying the invertebrate to understand the complex relationships between kelp forests, sea otters, sea urchins, sea stars and crabs.

Joshua Smith, a PhD student at the University of California, Santa Cruz, wanted to find out what happened and what role sea otters had played. He and a team of other researchers tracked sea otters in Monterey Bay and recorded what they were eating and where. He found that sea otters were eating more urchins than ever before. So why were there urchin barrens? An accomplished scuba diver, Joshua visited the sites where sea otters were eating urchins. He wanted to know how many urchins were in the area and how healthy they were.

In kelp forests where there is lots of food, urchins are very healthy. They have highly nutritious gonads— the term for the urchin's reproductive glands—a delicacy appreciated by both sea otters and humans. When urchins become super abundant, there is no kelp to eat, so the urchins respond by slowing down their metabolism, which helps them survive for decades with very little food. As a result, these urchins are relatively empty inside and they lose their tasty appeal. Joshua and his team discovered that the sea otters chose to eat the healthiest, fattest and most delicious urchins in the remaining kelp forests and entirely ignored starved urchins in the barrens. Unlike in northern California, where the kelp forest has almost entirely disappeared in the absence of *both* sea otters and sunflower sea stars, in central California, where sea otters are present, there are still patches of kelp forest that exist next to urchin barrens.

While sea otters may not be able to get rid of urchin barrens all by themselves, without the help of smaller predators, they may at least help slow down the destruction of the remaining kelp forest in central California by intensely eating urchins there. This is an exciting time for

An urchin barren and a kelp forest meet in shallow waters off the west coast of Haida Gwaii, BC.
LYNN LEE

the scientists who study sea otters and the role of smaller predators in complex, interconnected ecosystems.

As they are returning to the places they once occupied a long time ago, sea otters and other apex predators surprise all of us with what they can do, how they transform the ecosystem around them and how they reveal the importance of the multiple connections that exist between different species. They tell us how much we still don't know about the natural world.

Sea otters not only influence ecosystems but also change people's lives, and today people are rediscovering how they can coexist with sea otters.

Although sea otters rarely walk on land, they can be at high risk when they do. In Moss Landing, CA, sea-otter-crossing signs have been installed in key locations to remind drivers that they should watch for sea otters.

SEA OTTER XING

15 MPH

4

Living with Sea Otters

With the near extinction of sea otters during the fur trade, our coastal ecosystems changed dramatically. Generations of people no longer knew what a world with sea otters looked like. But now sea otters are coming back and reclaiming their historic habitat. The changes these ecosystem superheroes bring with them have consequences for humans, who must relearn how to live with them. And though the fur trade has ended, the world is not always a safe place for sea otters. They face many threats, and it is our responsibility to make sure sea otters stay with us now and in the future.

SEA OTTERS VS HUMANS

While many people view the sea otters' return as a conservation success story, others are less happy about the return of sea otters. When sea otters were gone from the eastern North Pacific, humans developed

A sea otter's appetite can create a conflict with people who have an economic and/or cultural interest in shellfish.

fisheries for shellfish such as Dungeness crab, geoduck clams and red sea urchins, which they could sell all over the world, particularly in Asia, where these particular invertebrates are considered delicacies.

Those fisheries now face competition from sea otters, and conflicts between sea otters and the people whose livelihoods depend on shellfish are on the rise. Shellfish harvesting is particularly important, both economically and culturally, for Indigenous communities. When sea otters move into a particular area and devour the shellfish that the locals used to eat, this poses a real threat to the survival of these coastal communities.

In southeastern Alaska, the sea-otter population grew quickly after 413 animals were reintroduced in the late 1960s. Now there are over 25,000 sea otters in this region, and several fisheries no longer exist as a result. Sea otters eat the large sea urchins, which happen to be the ones fishermen want to harvest and sell. Urchin fishermen complain that they have lost millions of dollars in revenue.

Another invertebrate that has been negatively affected by sea otters is the sea cucumber. To find out how much

Commercial shellfish operations such as the Monterey Abalone Company in California rely on healthy giant kelp. The kelp is hand-harvested from beds around the Monterey Peninsula and fed to the red abalone.

Sea otters are meticulously clean. After eating, they wash themselves in the ocean, cleaning their coats with their teeth and paws.

of an impact the sea otters are having, in 2010 and 2011 researchers compared sites with sea otters to sites without. They found that while the density of sea cucumbers declined in all areas, whether there were sea otters or not, the decline was four times greater in the places where sea otters had lived since at least 1994 than in the areas that had no sea otters. Where sea otters had existed since at least 2003 the decline was five times greater than at those sites without sea otters. Over time, the presence of the sea otters resulted in the closure of several sea-cucumber fisheries.

This means fishermen have to adapt, abandon certain activities, learn to live with sea otters and find new sources of income. This new reality is hard for people to accept, especially when the sea otters first come back.

In southeast Alaska, in fact, some people have asked that more hunting be allowed to control sea otters.

California sea cumbers (*Parastichopus californicus*), are negatively affected by an expanding sea-otter population in southeast Alaska. JAYAKESAVAN/GETTY IMAGES

IN THE FIELD:
Memories of a time without sea otters

Shellfish have always been an important source of food for Indigenous communities. Many people say that when the tide is out, the table is set. A few years ago I had the honor of meeting Hilda Hansen, a 94-year-old Kyuquot-Checleset First Nations Elder at her home in the village of Kyuquot. She remembered the time before sea otters were reintroduced to the region, when she could go to the beach with a bucket and pick up clams every day. There were many clams then, but Hilda says the sea otters came and destroyed everything, eating all the clams. "That was our food," she says.

In Tofino—another area on Vancouver Island where the sea otters have come back—I met with Joe Martin, a Nuu-chah-nulth canoe carver. Joe also remembers that when the sea otters first came back, they disrupted the clam beds, the crabs and the sea urchins. "I haven't eaten a sea urchin in a long time," he says.

Hilda Hansen remembers picking up clams on the beach before sea otters were reintroduced to the region.

When sea otters returned to British Columbia, their appetite for shellfish affected the livelihoods of coastal communities such as Kyuquot, on the west coast of Vancouver Island.

IN THE FIELD:
Ancient evidence

How do we learn from the past when nobody is alive to tell us how people used to coexist with sea otters before they were hunted to the brink of extinction? Luckily, archaeological **middens**—buried piles of shells and animal bones that were left behind by coastal inhabitants thousands of years ago—provide a great window into history. You have to look carefully under grass and shrubs to find this well-hidden organic compost, which is sometimes many feet deep and up to half a mile (0.8 kilometers) long. Middens hold precious treasures and are a key to understanding the past. They contain stone tools, shells, bones and other items that reveal how people lived and ate a very long time ago.

There are thousands of midden sites along the Pacific coast. In 2012 Iain McKechnie, an archaeologist at the University of Victoria in British Columbia, was part of a team that identified sea-otter bones dating back 5,000 years and examined the chemical signature of the bones. They found that the sea otters had a stable diet rich in shellfish, hinting that the locals were probably keeping the sea otters in check. The team reached this conclusion because studies in Alaska have shown that when there are lots of sea otters, there is less shellfish for them to eat. At the same time, because of the sea otters' presence, kelp is more abundant, which in turn supports more fish. As a result, fish becomes an important part of the sea otters' diet. When Iain looked at the ancient sea-otter bones and discovered that their diets relied mostly on invertebrates and not as much fish, it meant that there were fewer sea otters, which suggests that First Nations communities hunted sea otters to protect their clam-digging beaches.

Iain, other scientists and the Haida, Heiltsuk, Nuu-chah-nulth and Tsimshian Peoples hope to understand these ancient management practices so they can help resolve the modern conflicts between people and sea otters. They hope people can find ways to live with the sea otters and still be able to collect food from local shellfish beds.

A shell-midden site on Galiano Island, BC.
ERICA ELLEFSEN/ALAMY STOCK PHOTO

Archie Vincent, with grandson Xavier Short, is a fisherman who lives in Kyuquot. When sea otters gather in the shelter of kelp beds inside the reefs, he knows it's going to storm.

LEARNING TO LIVE WITH SEA OTTERS AGAIN

Prior to the fur trade during the 18th and 19th centuries, sea otters and Indigenous Peoples had lived in balance for thousands of years. The kelp forest—supported by a healthy population of sea otters—served as a "highway" for people traveling on the water and as a safe anchorage for boats. For the Alutiiq people of southern coastal Alaska, sea otters and people were one and the same. According to Alutiiq legends, the original sea otter was a man trapped by an incoming tide, who transformed into a sea otter to save himself.

Traditionally, Indigenous Peoples highly valued sea otters and used their fur in many ways. Chiefs and other high-ranking people wore ceremonial robes and adornments made out of sea-otter pelts. They used the fur for bedding and insulation. Sea-otter hunting was a respected skill in Indigenous communities. Only certain people were granted the privilege of hunting, and at specific times of the year.

Archaeological records and oral histories show that Indigenous Peoples managed sea-otter populations in their territories, excluding the animals from certain beaches so they could continue to collect shellfish for the benefit of their communities. It is thought that in Alaska and British Columbia, sea otters existed in lower numbers near village sites, where the important shellfish beds were, and in greater numbers along coastlines far from centers of human occupation. People may have used dogs to scare sea otters away, and hunters may have targeted the more adventurous male sea otters, since they are the ones that typically expand their territory.

Today Indigenous Peoples from Alaska are allowed to hunt sea otters. There's a provision in the US Marine Mammal Protection Act that recognizes the important connection between Indigenous Peoples and marine mammals. However, there is also a focus on conservation. Sea otters are carefully tagged, populations are monitored and sea-otter pelts must be made into goods before they can be sold. The Alaska Sea Otter and Steller Sea Lion Commission helps protect the customary and traditional uses of sea otters by the Indigenous Peoples in Alaska by promoting co-management, conservation, research, education and artistic development.

Sea-otter pelts are traditionally crafted into ceremonial robes and adornments, worn by Chiefs and other high-ranking people.
TERI ROFKAR (TLINGIT AND AMERICAN, 1956–2016), *CONTINUUM ROBE*, 2009, SEA OTTER FUR AND NATURAL DYES ON WOOL, 65 IN X 53 IN, PORTLAND ART MUSEUM, OREGON. MUSEUM PURCHASE: FUNDS PROVIDED BY NATIVE AMERICAN COUNCIL AND NATIVE AMERICAN ACQUISITIONS FUND, 2012.128.1a

A northern sea otter grooms itself after eating.

COULD THERE BE MORE FOR ALL?

While people who harvest shellfish may at first be upset by what they lose to sea otters when the animals come back, sea otters may actually provide greater benefits in the long term, not only to the local ecosystem, but also to humans. As a matter of fact, some researchers are trying to calculate what humans can expect to gain from the return of sea otters. As people learn more about the benefits sea otters provide, they may be able to forgive them for stealing a little bit of their dinner.

As you now know, sea otters revive kelp forests, which are nurseries for all kinds of fish species that people also eat. Edward Gregr, a researcher at the University of British Columbia, noted a 30 to 40 percent increase in living *biomass*—the total mass of organisms in an area—in places such as Kyuquot, where the number of sea otters is very high. This means more food is available to larger fish species such as halibut and salmon, which are of great commercial value to people.

Sea-Otter Watching

The return of sea otters can benefit tourism. The money that visitors spend to view wildlife in places like southeast Alaska or California can offset the loss of income from harvesting fewer shellfish.

A study conducted in 2010 on the west coast of Vancouver Island showed that a chance to see the charismatic sea otter was the second-most important factor—after seeing whales—in visitors' decisions to go on wildlife tours on Vancouver Island in British Columbia.

Morro Bay in California used to have an important abalone fishery. There are no more abalone to harvest, but sea otters have become a major tourist attraction in that area, and people now make money by running sea-otter-watching tours. Many of the fishermen who were angry when the sea otters first returned have now retired. The younger fishermen have a different view of fisheries and welcome the presence of sea otters, realizing there is more value in an ecosystem with sea otters than in one without them.

Ryan Sabbas, a Kyuquot/Checleset member, guides kayak tours in sea-otter territory.

IN THE FIELD:
Ecotourism and sea otters

David Pinel has made sea-otter viewing a main focus of the land-based and kayak tours he has led for more than 20 years on Vancouver Island. His business is co-owned with his wife, Caroline Fisher, and Bev Michel from the Kyuquot/Checleset First Nations. They hire members of the local Indigenous community so that they also have the opportunity to benefit from sea-otter related tourism. David tells tour participants, as they watch sea otters grooming, resting and eating, how the environment has changed over time and how the relationships between sea otters and humans have evolved. He also trains younger members of the local community to become guides.

Ryan Sabbas, Hilda Hansen's grandson, guides tours with David and is a graduate of the Aboriginal Ecotourism Training Program at a local college. Ryan, who is in his 20s, says he doesn't mind the sea otters and does not have the same negative feelings about them that his grandmother did.

Since sea otters arrived in Elkhorn Slough, they have become a major tourist attraction. Wildlife viewing should always be done responsibly. Give sea otters space—at least five kayak lengths.

A sea-otter-crossing sign and a speed bump were installed on Moss Landing Road, CA, to reduce sea-otter mortality.

As some people continue to adjust to the reality of the sea otters' return, the animals themselves are facing a variety of threats to their well-being, from predator attacks to pollution and climate change.

Too Close to People

Because sea otters live in coastal areas, they are often in contact with humans. Even though they live in the water, sea otters can be affected by humans' activities on land. Sea otters are susceptible to parasites coming from different sources. In California, waste from both domestic and wild cats, such as bobcats and mountain lions, carries a parasite called *Toxoplasma gondii*. If sea otters come into contact with this parasite when it enters the water, they get sick.

Fertilizer, *pesticides* and industrial chemicals get washed into the ocean and can end up in sea otters through the water or through the shellfish they eat. Over time sea otters become weaker and are more likely to get sick or be killed by infections.

You read in chapter 3 how an excess of nutrients in agricultural runoff spurs the growth of algae on seagrass leaves, blocking the sunlight the plants need. Those nutrients can also cause algae to grow rapidly and form patches on the surface of the water. These *algal blooms* produce toxins that can affect the health of animals and humans. One of the toxins released during harmful blooms is domoic acid, which accumulates in shellfish such as crabs and clams and in small fish. When humans and marine mammals eat contaminated shellfish or fish, the dangerous toxin affects their brains and can even cause death.

Because sea otters consume the same shellfish we like to eat, and shellfish are sensitive to marine pollution, sea otters act as sentinels for the health of our coasts. Melissa Miller is a veterinarian with the California Department of Fish and Wildlife. Her job is to understand what kills sea otters. She performs *necropsies*—detailed postmortem examinations of dead sea otters—to determine the cause of death. Her team maintains a catalog of details about every dead sea otter that washes up on the beaches of California, including the diseases that have affected them.

A few years ago Melissa discovered that 21 sea otters had died of microcystin intoxication. The toxin was produced by an algal bloom that originated in a freshwater lake and traveled downstream to the ocean, where it was absorbed by the shellfish that the sea otters ate. The discovery was a wake-up call for water authorities. In response to the scientific data provided by the researchers, they took steps to clean up the lake.

Sea otters are like a mirror, showing us the impact of the things we put in the water. As an indicator species, sea otters help us discover health threats that affect us all, both on land and in the ocean.

The Death Sentence of Oil Spills

On March 24, 1989, the *Exxon Valdez* ran aground in northwest Prince William Sound, Alaska. The ship spilled almost 11 million gallons (more than 40 million liters) of crude oil, contaminating more than 1,300 miles (2,100 kilometers) of shoreline. The oil spill killed fish, seabirds and marine mammals, including thousands of sea otters.

Sea otters are especially vulnerable to oil spills. When they come into contact with oil, their fur gets matted, which prevents it from insulating their bodies. Without this natural protection from the cold water, sea otters can quickly die from hypothermia (a condition defined as a dangerous drop in body temperature). Oil's toxicity is also harmful to sea otters, causing liver and kidney failure and damage to their lungs and eyes. Facilities to rescue sea otters were developed after the *Exxon* spill, but few oiled sea otters can ever be saved. Another oil spill could wipe out an entire population of sea otters if they were concentrated in the spill area.

Shark Attacks

Since the early 2000s, great white shark attacks on sea otters have dramatically increased in California. In fact, shark attacks are now the main cause of sea-otter death in this region, and shark-bitten animals account for more than half of the sea-otter carcasses that wash up on beaches. People are worried sea otters will be unable to expand their range in the north and the south of California and fully recover as a species.

Sharks don't eat sea otters when they attack them— they just bite. This may be because sharks eat fish when

Great white shark attacks are the main cause of sea-otter deaths in California.
JEFF ROTMAN/GETTY IMAGES

A group of sea otters snooze on their backs, showing their hind legs, tail and webbed feet, all of which make sea otters great swimmers.
GOMEZDAVID/GETTY IMAGES

they are young and then, after the first few years, move to marine mammals with lots of fat, such as seals and sea lions. But they have to learn to identify the right prey, and they may slip up. A young shark may mistake a sea otter for an elephant seal and take a bite, only to discover the prey is just an unappetizing fur ball with no fat. The shark moves on. Unfortunately, it is too late for the sea otter. One shark bite is all it takes to kill a sea otter.

Orca Attacks

In the 1990s, the number of sea otters living in the Aleutian Islands unexpectedly and suddenly decreased by 90 percent. Jim Estes—the biologist who had discovered the positive impact of sea otters on kelp forests in the 1970s—was the first to notice the sea otters' disappearance. He saw again that as the sea-otter population declined, urchins came back on the seafloor, and kelp forests began to vanish. Why were sea otters disappearing?

It turned out that mammal-eating orcas had suddenly decided to add sea otters to their dinner menu. But why

An orca is harassing a sea otter in Glacier Bay National Park, AK.
MTNMICHELLE/GETTY IMAGES

would they eat sea otters? Prior to 1991 there had been no confirmed attacks by orcas on sea otters, so the discovery was puzzling. To try to understand what had happened, Jim looked at the past and at other species in the region. He found that harbor seal populations were the first to collapse in the 1970s and '80s, followed by fur seals and sea lions and finally sea otters. What had caused this?

Jim and another colleague, Alan Springer, discovered that commercial whaling in the region after the Second World War was responsible for this chain reaction. Before humans started hunting whales on a large scale, mammal-eating orcas in the North Pacific and the southern Bering Sea could easily survive on a diet made up of whales. Once humans started to hunt the whales, things changed. By the time commercial whaling was stopped, there were no more whales left for the orcas to eat. As a result, the orcas were forced to change their diet. First they ate seals and sea lions, and then they switched to sea otters.

This remarkable chain reaction shows the immense impact that humans have had on the ecosystem through the overexploitation of animals. By hunting great whales, humans influenced the whole food chain, from top to bottom—from great whales, orcas, seals, sea lions and sea otters all the way down to urchins and kelp forests. These impacts still resonate though the entire ecosystem of a region and remind us yet again that everything is connected.

Climate Change

Climate change affects sea otters in various ways. Increased rainfall can produce more runoff from land, transporting more harmful *contaminants* to the marine environment. Rising ocean temperatures can spread disease among marine organisms, with potentially negative effects on sea otters. For example, toxic algal blooms may occur more frequently, placing sea otters at higher risk of exposure to domoic acid.

Scientists are also studying how *ocean acidification*— changes in the chemistry of the oceans due to excessive carbon dioxide in the atmosphere—may pose a threat

Sea otters spend most of their lives at sea, though they do occasionally get out of the water and clumsily walk on land.

to shellfish, many of which are important food for sea otters. When the water becomes more acidic, many invertebrates—clams, oysters, mussels, snails—have greater difficulty forming and maintaining their shells, and they die as a result.

HELPING SEA OTTERS

Throughout history sea otters have shown their incredible *resilience* and ability to survive, but how much more can they take? How will they adapt to climate change, increasing pollution and predator attacks? We have a responsibility to pay attention to the threats in the sea otters' environment and take the necessary steps to help sea otters survive in a fast-changing world.

Humans to the Rescue

When sea otters get in trouble, humans can help. In June 2017 a male sea-otter pup was found swimming alone without his mother in waters off northern Vancouver Island. Newborn sea otters are helpless without their mothers and are unable to survive without human intervention. This pup was estimated to be two to four weeks old when he was rescued and taken to the Vancouver Aquarium Marine Mammal Rescue Centre. Staff named him Hardy and cared for him 24 hours a day.

Over time, with the loving help of aquarium staff and volunteers who worked in rotating shifts on feeding, bathing and grooming the tiny pup, Hardy gained weight and became stronger. I was able to visit Hardy as he was recovering. It was hard not to fall in love with the tiny, fuzzy-faced pup that looked like a plush toy. I loved watching him play, feed, explore his underwater environment and

A curious sea otter approaches visitors at the Vancouver Aquarium.

interact with the attentive staff. Unfortunately, Hardy could not be released into the wild because he had not learned the essential skills from his mother that would allow him to survive on his own. He now lives permanently at the Vancouver Aquarium with other sea otters.

The Monterey Bay Aquarium in California has a program that rescues stranded sea-otter pups and introduces them to one of their non-releasable female sea otters, who serve as surrogate mothers. The pups have little contact with humans and do not get used to them. The surrogate moms teach the pups the skills they need to survive in the wild, such as grooming and foraging. When the pups are ready, the aquarium biologists release them into Elkhorn Slough and track them for years, collecting data on how well they do, how long they live and how many offspring they have.

Vancouver Aquarium staff and volunteers are feeding Hardy, a rescued sea-otter pup.

Rosa is the Monterey Bay Aquarium's oldest sea otter. She was found stranded in September 1999, only about four weeks old and weighing just over 5 pounds (2.2 kilograms). In April 2000 she was released back into the wild, where she lived for nearly two years. Then she began interacting with divers and climbing onto kayaks. Because of the potential risks to herself and people, wildlife managers declared her non-releasable, and she joined the aquarium's sea-otter exhibit. During her years at the aquarium, she has reared more pups than any other surrogate mom.

Coexisting with Sea Otters

In California, sea otters encounter humans frequently, especially in harbors and estuaries, where they are tourist attractions. In such places they are in danger of being disturbed by people coming too close and by boat traffic.

The Sea Otter Savvy program was established in the summer of 2015 to help reduce human disturbance of sea otters and to promote responsible wildlife viewing. Sea Otter Savvy members teach kayakers and boaters to stay a safe distance away from the sea otters so they do not interrupt the animals' eating and resting activities. When boaters approach an eating or resting sea otter, the animal will dive to get away. That takes energy a sea otter cannot afford to waste, and over time it can affect the sea otter's survival, particularly if the animal is a female with pups. Researchers have found that in Elkhorn Slough, sea otters are forced to dive up to 20 times per day because of boaters. Scientists have discovered that a sea otter who is forced to expend energy diving and swimming away from humans six times a day has to eat nine extra clams to make up for the disturbance. We can all enjoy watching sea otters from a distance.

What Can You Do to Help Sea Otters?

Spread the learning! Keep learning about sea otters and talk to others about these ecosystem superheroes. Discuss the important role that sea otters and other top predators play in the environment. Many people do not understand the critical function that predators such as sea otters, wolves and cougars perform in their ecosystem, and how these animals benefit many other species, including humans. People sometimes have a hard time coexisting with predators, which has resulted in predators being misunderstood and persecuted in different parts of the world. With your new knowledge, you can help educate others about the value of predators such as sea otters and why they should be protected.

In places where sea otters have returned, their presence sets the stage for opportunities to view diverse wildlife, from the smallest invertebrates in the intertidal zone to rich kelp forests.

Understanding the needs of sea otters is important to help prevent disturbances. When people get too close to sea otters, this can cause them stress, waste their energy and be harmful to their health.

Moss Landing State Beach

Please Do Not Disturb Sea Otters

- Sea otters are threatened marine mammals. When you approach them when they are resting on land you are harassing them. Marine mammals are protected by law.
- Keep a distance between you and the sea otter of at least 50 yards.
- To report people harassing sea otters call the Department of Fish and Wildlife at:
- Call Cal-TIP: 1-888-334-2258

Por Favor no Molestar a las Nutrias Marinas

- Las nutrias marinas son mamíferos marinos amenazados. Cuando están descansando en tierra y usted se acerca a ellos los está molestando. Los mamíferos marinos están protegidos por la ley.
- Mantenga una distancia de por lo menos 50 yardas entre usted y la nutria marina.
- Para reportar a personas hostigando las nutrias marinas llame a el Departamento de Peces y Vida Silvestre al:
- Cal-TIP: 1-888-334-2258

CALIFORNIA STATE PARKS

Volunteer! In different areas where sea otters are present, scientists need volunteers to help them monitor the animals' behavior. On the central California coast, for example, the Sea Otter Savvy program often needs citizen scientists to observe sea otters with binoculars or a spotting scope and record information about them. The data you collect will help protect sea otters in California. Look for similar opportunities where you live. You can also volunteer to help maintain a healthy and clean marine environment for sea otters. Assist with a beach cleanup, for example, or join an organization engaged in ocean conservation. Many wildlife species become endangered because of habitat loss and degradation. Think about ways you can help protect a natural area near your home—such as a salt marsh—and support habitat restoration at nearby waterways.

Respect sea-otter space! When you are watching a sea otter in its environment, be respectful and maintain a safe distance. Sea otters that are frequently exposed to

Volunteers observe southern sea otters in California and record data on their behavior. The information they collect will contribute to a better understanding and protection of the species.

We all have a role to play to help protect the coastal environment that we share with sea otters.

humans can get used to people, which results in a loss of fear, increased boldness and, in some cases, aggression toward humans and pets. This is not something we want, as it always ends up badly for the sea otters.

Be aware of your activities on land! What we do on a daily basis can affect sea otters. Think about sea otters as neighbors in your community. Even if you do not live in an area close to sea otters, you are connected to them through the ocean environment we are all part of. When you look after sea otters, you contribute to healthier ecosystems and communities. Reduce, reuse and recycle whenever you can. Stop using plastic bags, straws and water bottles—they pollute the ocean and kill marine life. Ask your parents to use nontoxic household cleaning products and to purchase sustainable, recycled, biodegradable goods. Eat organic food, produced with no pesticides or fertilizers. Eat less or no meat to reduce greenhouse gases. Do not litter, and be aware of everything your family puts down the drain, since most of it will eventually make its way into rivers, streams and oceans. Remember that sea otters are affected by agricultural pesticides and even flushable cat litter! Learn about climate change and how you can do your part.

IN THE FIELD:
Getting sea otters to the other side of the road

Watching a sea otter cross the road is an unusual sight, but it happens. The community of Moss Landing sits at the mouth of Elkhorn Slough where about 100 sea otters live. Below Moss Landing Road are culverts that allow sea otters to swim from the harbor to the slough when they are looking for food. At high tide, tidal gates close to keep salt water out of the slough, and the sea otters cannot swim between the two areas. When the gates close, the sea otters have only one option: they have to get out of the water and walk across Moss Landing Road to get from the harbor to the slough. Unfortunately, the road is busy, and it is difficult to spot sea otters crossing the road.

One evening, volunteer Ron Eby and I monitored a sea otter that was getting ready to cross the road. On land sea otters move slowly and awkwardly, which is dangerous when they are crossing roads. During the time I was with Ron, he never took his eyes off the sea otter and was prepared to stop traffic when the sea otter wanted to cross. He had reason to be worried. In the summer of 2016, a male sea otter crossing Moss Landing Road was hit by a car and died. He had been named Mr. Enchilada by locals because he always hung out in the harbor near The Whole Enchilada restaurant and a walking path frequently used by tourists.

After Mr. Enchilada died, a speed bump was installed on Moss Landing Road to slow down vehicle traffic. Sea-otter-crossing signs indicating a lowered speed limit were also installed in key locations along the road.

In the end, the sea otter I monitored with Ron safely crossed the road late at night, but it is important that drivers in areas such as these slow down and watch for sea otters so they can get across the road safe and sound.

Volunteer Ron Eby is watching for traffic on Moss Landing Road so that a sea otter can safely cross the road from the harbor to Elkhorn Slough.

Researchers have found that kelp forests are nearly 20 times larger on the west coast of Vancouver Island, BC, where sea otters are present.

AN UNFINISHED STORY

Sea otters are extraordinary animals. They have a major influence on their environment, and they help restore important ecosystems, which benefits other species. They have taught scientists many lessons about how the natural world works.

Sea otters also remind us of the vital role predators play in maintaining healthy ecosystems. Unfortunately, humans continue to wage war against predators such as gray wolves, lions and cougars, seeing them as a threat to themselves and/or their livelihoods. Throughout the world, large carnivores are experiencing massive population declines because of human greed and habitat loss. The return of a predator such as the sea otter shows us why it is important to protect and value all predators in ecosystems. Scientists are learning how predators affect food chains, heal damaged environments and ultimately help preserve a delicate natural balance that benefits many species, including us.

As for sea otters, their story continues. There will be a lot more to learn from them as they continue to reclaim their territories.

A sea otter settles in for a nap in a patch of kelp.

Glossary

activity budget—how much time an animal spends on various behaviors throughout the day, such as eating, sleeping, traveling and socializing

algal bloom—a rapid increase in the growth of algae in an aquatic system

biomass—the total mass of living organisms in an area

carbon dioxide—an invisible, colorless gas formed by burning fuels, the breaking down or burning of animal or plant matter, and the act of breathing; it is absorbed from the air by plants during photosynthesis

carbon sink—an area that absorbs carbon dioxide and keeps it out of the atmosphere

carnivore—an animal that feeds on meat

citizen science—scientific data collection and analysis undertaken by members of the general public, often in collaboration with or under the direction of professional scientists and scientific institutions

climate change—changes in the world's weather patterns, particularly a rise in temperature, thought to be caused by such things as increased levels of carbon dioxide in the atmosphere produced by the use of fossil fuels

contaminant—any potentially undesirable substance (physical, chemical or biological) that makes something impure; usually refers to the introduction of harmful human-made substances

ecosystem—a complex network involving all living organisms interacting with the nonliving components of their environment

end-lactation syndrome—a condition that can develop in a female sea otter that means she provides more energy to her pup than she can physiologically afford to provide, leaving her very emaciated and weakened by the time the pup is old enough to wean

estuary—a body of water where fresh water and salt water meet

extinction—the disappearance of a species from the earth

food chain—a series of living things that are linked to one another because each feeds on the next; many connected food chains make up a food web

habitat—the place where plants, animals and other organisms normally live and breed

herbivore—an animal that eats plants

holdfast—a rootlike structure that allows seaweed to attach to something hard, such as a rock

indicator species—an organism that serves as a measure of the environmental conditions in a specific area

intertidal zone—the area of the marine shoreline that is exposed to air at low tide and covered by seawater at high tide

invertebrate—an animal that does not have a spine

kelp—a large brown seaweed that grows in cold coastal waters, consisting of a holdfast that anchors the plant to the ocean floor, a stipe or stem-like structure, and a blade or leaf-like appendage

keystone species—a species that has a major influence on the way an ecosystem works such that if it were removed, the ecosystem would change drastically

midden—a deposit of shells, animal bones and other garbage that indicates the site of a human settlement

nearshore—broadly defined as the region extending from the shoreline to a location just beyond where the waves break

necropsy—the examination of a dead animal, particularly to determine the cause of death

nutrient—a substance that provides nourishment to promote growth and maintain life

ocean acidification—a change in the chemistry of the ocean caused by carbon dioxide being absorbed by the ocean reacting with the seawater and producing acid; it is caused primarily by excess carbon dioxide in the atmosphere

pesticide—a chemical used to kill pests, such as insects, that damage crops

pollution—the presence of harmful chemicals or other substances in the environment

predator—an animal that hunts other animals for food; an apex predator is the top animal in a food chain

prey—an animal that is hunted and eaten by other animals

raft—a group of sea otters floating on the water to rest

range—the native geographic area in which an organism can be found; the geographic distribution of a particular species

remnant population—a small surviving group

resilience—the capacity to withstand change and recover from damage or disturbance

seagrass—a flowering plant that has adapted to live in the marine environment

sediment—stones, sand and other material carried by water or wind and deposited into rivers and onto the ocean floor

shellfish—an aquatic invertebrate animal with a shell

site fidelity—the tendency of an animal to remain in an area over an extended period or to return to an area previously occupied

species—a group of closely related organisms that share similar characteristics and are capable of producing offspring

trophic cascade—a series of interactions through which the top predator in a food chain can affect the entire ecosystem by its impact on its prey and, indirectly, its prey's prey; the word *trophic* relates to nutrition

urchin barren—an area in the marine environment where sea urchins have become the dominant species

Resources

PRINT

Druehl, Louis, and Bridgette Clarkston. *Pacific Seaweeds: A Guide to Common Seaweeds of the West Coast*. Madeira Park, BC: Harbour Publishing, 2016.

Eisenberg, Cristina. *The Wolf's Tooth: Keystone Predators, Trophic Cascades, and Biodiversity*. Washington, DC: Island Press, 2011.

Estes, James A. *Serendipity: An Ecologist's Quest to Understand Nature*. Oakland, CA: University of California Press, 2016.

Larson, Shawn E., James L. Bodkin and Glenn R. VanBlaricom, eds. *Sea Otter Conservation*. Cambridge, MA: Academic Press (an imprint of Elsevier), 2015.

Mapes, Lynda V., and Alan Berner. *Rescuing Rialto: A Baby Sea Otter's Story*. New York: Roaring Brook Press, 2019.

McLeish, Todd. *Return of the Sea Otter: The Story of the Animal That Evaded Extinction on the Pacific Coast*. Seattle: Sasquatch Books, 2018.

Newman, Patricia. *Sea Otter Heroes: The Predators That Saved an Ecosystem*. Minneapolis: Millbrook Press, 2017.

Ravalli, Richard. *Sea Otters: A History*. University of Nebraska Press, 2018.

Stolzenburg, William. *Where the Wild Things Were: Life, Death, and Ecological Wreckage in a Land of Vanishing Predators*. New York: Bloomsbury USA, 2009.

Terborgh, John, and James A. Estes, eds. *Trophic Cascades: Predators, Prey, and the Changing Dynamics of Nature* (second edition). Washington, DC: Island Press, 2010.

ONLINE

Coastal Voices: coastalvoices.net

Elkhorn Slough National Estuarine Research Reserve: elkhornslough.org

Elkhorn Slough OtterCam: elkhornslough.org/ottercam

Monterey Bay Aquarium Sea Otter Cam: montereybayaquarium.org/
    animals-and-exhibits/live-web-cams/sea-otter-cam

Sea Otter Savvy: seaottersavvy.org

Seaotters.com

Acknowledgments

For over 10 years I have watched sea otters regain their territory in British Columbia. I have also observed sea otters in California and Alaska. During this time I have had ongoing conversations with the scientists who are studying sea otters and their impacts on the environment and the communities around them. Through the eyes of these scientists, I have come to appreciate a truly exciting journey of scientific exploration and learned that the natural world is full of surprises. This book is the result of that journey, and I am extremely grateful to all the individuals who over the years have generously shared their knowledge of and experiences with sea otters in different communities and invited me to join their field research.

In British Columbia, I thank Linda Nichol, Jane Watson, Anne Salomon, Josie Osborne, Jenn Burt, Erin Foster, Lynn Lee, Russell Markel, Rebecca Martone, Kai Chan, Margot Hessing-Lewis, Roger Dunlop, Joe Martin, Iain McKechnie, Edward J. Gregr and the Vancouver Aquarium.

I am especially indebted to David Pinel and his family, who generously hosted me several times in the territory of the Kyuquot/Checleset First Nations and introduced me to many people in the community of Kyuquot who kindly agreed to share their Traditional Knowledge of and experiences with sea otters.

In California, I thank Tim Tinker, Brent Hughes, Lilian Carswell, Ron Eby, James Estes, Michelle Staedler, Mark Carr, Peter Raimondi, Joshua Smith, Gena Bentall, Michael Harris, Joe Tomoleoni, Kerstin Wasson and the Monterey Bay Aquarium.

In Alaska, I thank Ginny Eckert and Daniel Monson.

I thank Orca Book Publishers for accepting a book on sea otters, and particularly my wonderful editors, Sarah Harvey and Kirstie Hudson, for their kindness, patience, insightful comments and support, and Dahlia Yuen, for her beautiful design. I thank Jenn Burt and Erin Foster for kindly taking the time to thoroughly review the manuscript for scientific accuracy and to provide thoughtful comments.

Lastly, my deepest thanks to my family, who always gave me support and encouragement when I needed it and kindly listened, with enthusiasm and curiosity, to my endless sea-otter stories.

Index

*Page numbers in **bold** indicate an image caption.*